MY

moshi monsters
™

JOKE BOOK

Where would you find the
best Moshi Monsters jokes?
In this book, silly!
Lovegirl14941

SUNBIRD
Published by Ladybird Books Ltd 2010
A Penguin Company
Penguin Books Ltd, 80 Strand, London, WC2R 0RL, UK
Penguin Group (USA) Inc., 375 Hudson Street, New York 10014, USA
Penguin Books Australia Ltd, Camberwell Road, Camberwell, Victoria 3124,
Australia (A division of Pearson Australia Group Pty Ltd)
Canada, India, New Zealand, South Africa

Sunbird is a trade mark of Ladybird Books Ltd

© Mind Candy Ltd. Moshi Monsters is a trademark of Mind Candy Ltd.
All rights reserved.

www.ladybird.com

ISBN: 978-1-40939-046-9

014

Printed in Great Britain by Clays Ltd, St Ives plc

MY moshi monsters™

JOKE BOOK

WITH OVER 230 MONSTER·TICKLING
JOKES SUBMITTED BY YOU!

Contents

Greetings, Monsters!

Welcome to the first ever Moshi Monsters joke book created by YOU! All the side-splitting, monster-tickling jokes within these pages were sent to *The Daily Growl* by the citizens of Monstro City.

It's a good thing I have so many eyes, because over 8,000 hilarious humdingers were sent in, and Yours Truly had to read each and every one of them. My eyes really came in handy (even when I wasn't holding them in my hands!). I was up all night, but somehow I managed to pick out my favourite funnies.

Check out the monsters who submitted the very best of the best on the colour pages. They're the ones that had me spewing Slop out of my nose. Unfortunately I was facing Tyra Fangs' closet. So guess what? Green is the IT colour this season. Heh.

You can keep the jokes coming over at the Moshi Forum. Just visit **http://forums. moshimonsters. com** to submit.

Keep your eyes at hand...

Roary Scrawl

FIRST JOKE POSTED!

Why did Roary Scrawl cross the road?

To get to his other eyes!
Funker29

7

Monster Mayhem

What do you do if you see a monster?
Run!
Princessrhi-rhi

What is the best way to speak to an angry monster?
From a long way away!
Supersweet47

On which day do monsters eat people?
Chewsday!
Cuddlyxbear

What does a polite monster say when he meets you for the first time?
Pleased to eat you!
Bluedawg

What do monsters make with cars?
Traffic jam!
Candy51129

Where can you find a really ugly monster?
Take a look in the mirror!
Petparty2

How do Moshi Monsters wash their clothes?
In a washing Moshine!
Verymelanie

That girl monster just rolled her eyes at me.

Well, roll them back, she might need them!
Pinkalive

9

Furi Funnies

What do you get if you come across a Furi with his eyes closed?
Squashed!
Llooonnyy

What do you call Furi with no fur?
I.
Graciemycat

Why is Furi's hand only 11 inches long?
Because if it was 12 inches, it would be a foot!
Olivia807

What's big, fierce, furry and has eight wheels?

Furi on roller skates!

Hellokittyfan1

What's as big as Furi but doesn't weigh anything?

Furi's shadow!

5jess5

What do you call an angry monster?

FURIous!

Mary241211

Why did Furi eat the lightbulb?

He wanted a light snack!

Leafdapple9

What's big, hairy and bounces up and down?

A Furi on a pogo stick!

Lavacane

Knock, Knocks!

Knock, knock!
Who's there?
Boo.
Boo who?
Don't cry, it's only a joke!
Angelmouase1

Knock, knock!
Who's there?
Furi.
Furi who?
I'm Furious you don't remember me!
Lilo755

Knock, knock!
Who's there?
Ice cream.
Ice cream who?
Ice cream if you don't let me in!
Nickko

Knock, knock!
Who's there?
Police.
Police who?
Police stop telling these awful knock, knock jokes!
Chivasfan2010

Will you remember me in a minute?
Yes.
Will you remember me in an hour?
Yes.
Will you remember me in a day?
Yes.
Just get on with it!
Will you remember me in a week?
Yes.
A month?
Yes.
A year?
YES!
Knock, knock.
Who's there?
You've forgotten me already!
Connymae

MOSHLING MANIA

What's black and white and goes round and round?
Peppy in a revolving door.
Johnny222789

What did Jeepers say to the flea?
Stop bugging me!
Filatoff

What do you call a pink IGGY?
Piggy.
Sweetlolipoplover

What is DJ Quack's favourite food?
Quackers!
Cade07

What kind of music does Scamp the Froggy Doggy like?
Hip hop!
Leny449670

What's the difference between Blurp and a piano?
You can't tune a fish!
Pumpkinpy

Why did Hansel cross the road?
Gretel was on the other side.
Brandypop

What did Cleo say to Rocky the Baby Blockhead?
You rock!
mella84

LUVLI Laughs!

What is Luvli's favourite soap opera?
Beastenders!
Pingy

Why did Luvli keep her trumpet in the fridge?

Because she liked cool music!
Onecoolangel

Why is getting up at 4am like Luvli's antenna?
Because it's twirly!
1purpleboots1

Did you catch everyone's eye in that dress, dear?

Yes, mum, and I've brought them all home for cousin Zommer to use!
Mifs1

Why are you so late?

I stopped to smell a brose.

There's no B in rose.

There was in that one!
Lightlily12

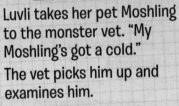

Luvli takes her pet Moshling to the monster vet. "My Moshling's got a cold."

The vet picks him up and examines him.

"I'm sorry Luvli, I'm going to have to put him down."

"Why? Because he's got a cold?"

"No," says the vet, "because he's too heavy!"

Neil0901

WHAT'S A CHICKEN DOING IN A BOOK ABOUT MONSTERS?

Why **didn't** the chicken cross the road?

Because he was a chicken!

Pokemonlover1612

Why did the turkey cross the road?

To prove he wasn't a chicken!

Moshi-megsta

Why did the chewing gum cross the road?

It was stuck to the chicken's foot!

Bramble30

Why did Poppet cross the road?

Because it was the chicken's day off!

Izzyzara

Why did Diavlo cross the road?
Zommer had tied him to the chicken!
Lydia4030

Why did the monster cross the road?
Because it was hungry for chicken!
Zazzbaa

Why did the chicken join the band?
Because it had a great pair of drumsticks!
Cutey4226

Why did Doris cross the road?
Because the chicken hadn't been invented yet!
Ajlawless01

Why did Oddie cross the road?
To get away from the chicken.
Lucky173

Party Pieces

Why didn't the skeleton go to the party?
Because he had no body to go with!
Kittyprinsess

Why did the mushroom go to the party?
Because he was a fun guy!
Mizzeva211

What do monsters like most about parties?
The finger food!
Coolies3483

Why did Furi take toilet paper to a party?
Because he's a party pooper!
Lottierocks12

GHOULISH GAMES

What is Roary Scrawl's favourite game?
Eye spy!
Tussar

What's a monster's favourite game?
Swallow the leader!
Malaika2000

What's a monster's second favourite game?
Hide and shriek!
Gemmy4

Foodie Fun

Two sausages were frying in a pan. One jumps up and says, "My, it's hot in here." Then the other jumps up and says, "Wow! A talking sausage!"

Slippy10200

How do you make a monster float?

Take two scoops of ice cream, a glass of fizzy pop and add one monster!

Cococherry12345

What's a monster's favourite bean?

A human bean!

Sparklepie10

Where would you find a Moshi Monster at a concert?
In the Moshi pit!
Coochipie

What sits in custard looking miserable?
Apple grumble!
Luvebug6911

Did you hear about the accident at Gabby's Café last night?
Two sausages got battered!
Coracoco1234

GABBY'S CAFE

What's a monster's favourite food?
Boo-berries and I-scream!
Bunnyboo596

Waiter, waiter! There's a Moshling in my salad!
Don't yell it out, the other monsters will want one!
Shazacookie172

ZOMMER GIGGLES

What haircare product does Zommer use?
Scarespray!
Monsterannie

Why did Zommer cross the road?
To get to the second hand shop!
Abd-dbn

What time did Zommer go to the dentist?
2.30!
monika428

How can you tell if Zommer has a glass eye?
Because it comes out in conversation!
Bluedawg

THE FIZZBANGS

What do you call a Zommer who plays the drums?
A drommer!
Jet-ray-moshi

Does Zommer eat Slopcorn with his fingers?
No, he eats the fingers separately!
Ibreakurcrayons

What do you get when Zommer scares a cow?
A milkshake!
Northwesterngal

What did Zommer say to his sweetheart?
It was love at first fright!
Moshi_moshi0420

Why did Zommer wear two pairs of pants to go golfing?
In case he got a hole in one!
Maddogsing9

What's Zommer's favourite sport?
Snot-putt!
Lupocp12345

Captain Buck's Chuckles

What is the most dangerous vegetable to have on Captain Buck's boat?

A leek!

Laura3768

Why is Captain Buck a pirate?

Because he arrrrrrr!

Groovy-gracie

How much did it cost for Captain Buck to have his ears pierced?

A buck an ear!

Percyjacksonlover_x

Why couldn't the monster sailors play cards?

Captain Buck was standing on the deck!

Oomph2259

Why did Captain Buck cross the sea?

To get to the other tide!

Burpy09

What type of monsters live at the port?

Buoys and gulls!

Selgomez2010

Where does Captain Buck buy his Christmas presents?

Arrrrrrrrrrrgos!

Meggymoo157

What did Captain Buck say when the Furi stepped on his foot?

Arrrrrrrrrgh!

Mombo333

Katsuma Killers!

What do you call Katsuma with headphones on?

Anything you like, he can't hear you!

Hats300

Why did Katsuma blush when he opened the fridge?

Because he saw the Fly Trap Salad dressing!

Popcorn688

What did one of the Katsuma's eyes say to the other?

Something between us smells!

Kialn

I would tell you the joke about Katsuma's broken tooth, but there's no point to it...

Choccychip7

What colour is Katsuma on a roller coaster?
Green with stripes.

Bobbythedog

Why is the letter V like a Katsuma?
Because it comes after U!

Goodgirlgirl

Peppy was waddling down the road and Katsuma picked him up. A police monster told Katsuma to take Peppy to the Moshling zoo, so Katsuma did. The next day the police monster saw the same Katsuma walking by with Peppy. " I thought I told you to take him to the zoo." He said. "I did," Katsuma replied, "but today we're going to the Moshi Fun Park!"

Tas3000

What do you call a Katsuma in the Antarctic?
Lost!

Lauren21286934

MONSTER CHORTLES

A monster went to London on a horse. The monster left Monstro City on Friday. He went to London for three days and travelled back on Friday. How did he do it?

The horse's name was Friday!

Twinkle5rg

What did the monster eat after its teeth were pulled out?

The dentist!

Cuddlyxbear

What do sea monsters have for supper?

Fish and ships!

Iluvcookies379

What's big and ugly and goes up and down?
A monster in a lift.
Aymendaman

How do you stop a monster from smelling?
Cover its nose!
Kialn

What do you give a seasick monster?
Plenty of room!
Vipvampire

What do you do with a blue monster?
Try and cheer him up!
Percyjacksonlover_x

How do you stop a monster from digging up your garden?
Take his spade away!
Hellopello1

S'not Funny!

What do you call a green fly with no wings?
A bogey!
Toothygrinface

What's the difference between chocolate-coated broccoli and snot?
Monsters love eating snot!
9hippie9

What do you find in a clean nose?
Fingerprints!
Bubba0808

Why do Furi's have big nostrils?
Because they have big fingers!
Blueberry9242

What's black and white and black and white and black and white? **ShiShi rolling down a hill!**

News! Forum! Help! Membership!

MONSTAR LIST

LEVEL 5

VIEW PROFILE

10

MOOD

GIFT ROOM 1

HEALTH

PUZZLES

MY NEWS

HAPPINESS

ZOO

Stardust is feeling vivacious

FRIENDS

SCROLL

SCROLL

ROX 371

MONSTER OWNER addyris2

11

Friends: 9

RATE THIS ROOM ☆☆☆☆☆

Two Poppets are sitting in a field. One says to the other, "Are you worried about this mad monster sickness that's going around?" The other replies, "Nope, I'm a squirrel."

Why did Furi end up in hospital after busking on Main Street? Because all the other monsters threw Rox at him!

Knock, knock.
Who's there?
I'm a pile-up.
I'm a pile-up who?
He he he he!

USERNAME: TWILIGHT246218

Hansel: You can't catch me, I'm the gingerbread...
Zommer: Munch! Munch!
Zommer: What were you saying?

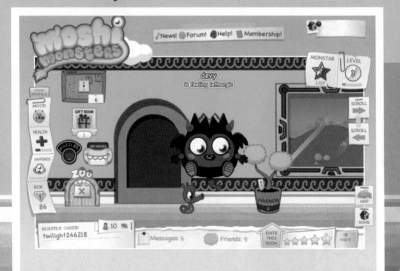

How do you keep a monster in suspense? I'll tell you tomorrow...

Katsuma: Can I lick the bowl?
Katsuma's mum: No, flush it like everyone else!

How do you make the Cluekoo dizzy? Chase it round the garden!

USERNAME: PUMPKINPY

What happened when White Fang lost his first tooth? The tooth Furi came!

USERNAME: SILLYSHERRY

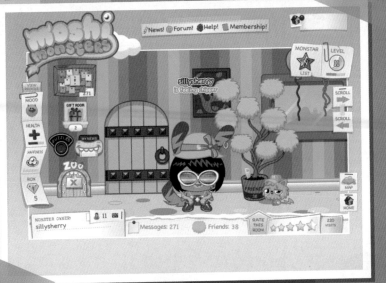

Furi walked into a shop and asked the shopkeeper for a fork, then he walked out. Katsuma walked into the same shop, asked for a fork as well then left. Another Furi walked in and did the same. Then Zommer walked in and asked for a straw. "I thought you'd want a fork, everyone else wanted one," said the shopkeeper. "Oh," said Zommer, "that's because a monster spewed on the sidewalk but all the chunky bits have gone."

Little monster: Mum, mum, what's for tea?
Mother monster: Shut up and get back in the microwave!

USERNAME: NOISYSKULL17

What do you get when you cross a Katsuma with a mutant sprout? I don't know, but it sounds dangerous!

HA! HA!

What does the Cluekoo use as a bookmark? A bookworm!

Emma8348

School Daze

What was the Diavlo known as at school?

A bright spark!

Dollface911

Why didn't Oddie take the bus home from school?

Because it wouldn't fit in his backpack!

Aby1013

Why would Roary Scrawl make a good teacher?

Because he's got eyes in the back of his head!

Abby924

Why didn't the monster want to go to his maths class?

Because he was too ghoul for school!

Smudgetastic

Why did Zommer give up being a teacher?

Because he only had one pupil!

Minimonstrosity

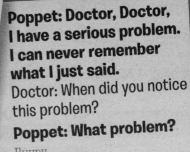

Poppet: Doctor, Doctor, I have a serious problem. I can never remember what I just said.
Doctor: When did you notice this problem?
Poppet: What problem?

Iluvny

Simon Growl walks into a doctor's office with a baby marrow up his nose, a cucumber in his left ear and a bread stick in his right ear.

"Doctor, what's wrong with me?" he asks.

"You're not eating right!" says the doctor.

psychochicken

Katsuma: Doctor, doctor, I think I'm a bridge.
Doctor: What's come over you?
Katsuma: Six cars, two trucks and a bus.

Fard

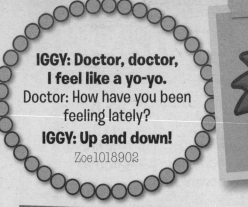

IGGY: Doctor, doctor, I feel like a yo-yo.
Doctor: How have you been feeling lately?
IGGY: Up and down!
Zoe1018902

Katsuma: Doctor, doctor, I think I need glasses!
Furi: You certainly do, this is the Gross-ery store!
Legofan246

Furi: Doctor, Doctor, I've eaten too much trashcan surprise!
Doctor: Don't talk rubbish!
Doggerdig08

Monster Tickles

Interviewer: Do you like children?

Monster: Oh, yes! I love children - boiled, fried, scrambled...

Mishi12556

How do monsters like their eggs?
Terror-fried!

5jess5

How do you spell monsters backwards?

MONSTERSBACKWARDS!

MushyFlowerGoo

What has a purple spotted body, ten hairy legs and big eyes on stalks?

I don't know either, but there's one crawling up your leg!

Pieromaneeac

Why did the monster stare at the orange juice for three hours?

Because it said "concentrate"!

Jordi7200

Why are monsters scared to go to sleep at night?

In case there's a human hiding under the bed!

321purple123

What steps should you take if an axe-wielding monster gallops towards you?

Great big ones!

Carly91290

What should you do if a monster smashes through your front door?

Run through the back door, fast!

Neon_neon

Why was Poppet's nose tired?

Because it never stopped running!

Volcane4066

What's pink and fluffy with mud on it?

Poppet rolling down a hill!

Vickimybfect

Which kind of Moshi Monster is good at singing?

Pop-pet!

Avatargirl12

Why did the Poppet cross the Moshi Fun Park?

To get to the other ride!

Awesomepossum9035

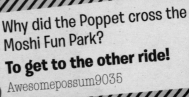

Toilet Humour

What did the monster say when he was flushed down the toilet?

Weeeeeeeeeeeeeeee!

Kels-88

Why did the toilet paper roll down the hill?

To get to the bottom!

Ambiemily1999

What's invisible and smells like garlic marshmallows?

Furi farts!

Emmy1465

A Katsuma, a Poppet and a Diavlo are travelling through the desert. They come across a magician and a slide. The magician says, "Whatever drink you call out when you go down the slide, you will land in a big pool of it."

So the Katsuma went down the slide and called out, "TOAD SODA!" He landed in a pool of Toad Soda.

Then the Poppet went down and called out, "Essence of Blue!" She landed in a pool of it.

Then the Diavlo went down the slide and shouted, "Weeeeeee!"

Oops!

Kuva09

If H_2O is on the inside of a fire hydrant, what is on the outside?

K9P!

Kawabata

What did one Monstro City public toilet say to the other?

You look a little flushed!

Stuffurface123

What's the difference between roast beef and pea soup?

You can roast beef but you can't pea soup!

Cedric1223

MOSHLING MERRIMENT

What do you call a happy Peppy?
A pen-grin!
Skite1306

What's the difference between IGGY and a cat?
Nothing, they both like chasing mice!
Cheese-on-toast

Why couldn't Angel sing?
Because she was a little horse!
Luciecherryxxx

How do you catch Chop Chop?
Act like a banana!
Peacebunny333

DJ Quack walked into a store and ordered a hamburger. When the waitress asked if he wanted to pay now, he said, "Just put it on my bill!"

Jbdavis

How does Ecto begin a fairy tale?

Once upon a slime...

Bluedawg

Where does Scamp the Froggy Doggy hang his coat?

In the croakroom!

Al5151

Why did Mini Ben jump out of a window?

To see time fly!

Greenwand

Diavlo Sniggers

Why did Diavlo eat his homework?
Because IGGY told him it was a piece of cake!
Piplup0218

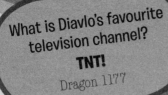

What is Diavlo's favourite television channel?
TNT!
Dragon1177

Why did Diavlo burn his homework?
Because his dog was full!
Moshishelly

What did Diavlo say when he sat on Hansel?
Oh, crumbs!
Annees1234

Someone told me that Diavlo invented matches.

Yes, that was one of his most striking achievements!

Bluedawg

Did you put the dog out?

I didn't know he was on fire!

Puffy-choochoo

Further Foodie Fun

What do Italian monsters like to eat?
Spook-ghetti!
Fuzzycat01

What's round, white and giggles?
A tickled onion!
1smilezallround1

What's green and dangerous?
Shark-infested slop!
Poppet317

Furi and Poppet were having dinner in the grungiest restaurant in town. "What's this fly doing in my slop?" Furi asked Poppet. "It looks like the backstroke to me!" she replied.

Hayleybayley1

ANIMAL ANTICS

What do you give sick pigs?
Oinkment!
Pokemon9061

What do you get if you walk under a cow?
A pat on the head!
Pinkcutie3004

What did the scientist say when he found bones on the moon?
Looks like the cow didn't make it!
Bree-tanner

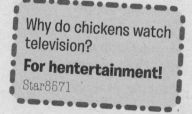

Why do chickens watch television?
For hentertainment!
Star8571

How do you make friends with a squirrel?
Climb up a tree and act like a nut!
Angellynea101

Freaky Funnies

Why are graveyards always so noisy?
Because of all the coffin!
Browser123

Why is 6 afraid of 7?
Because 7 8 9!
Princessrhi-rhi

What room has no doors, no windows, no floor and no walls?
A mushroom.
Maxmarquise69

What's green and sings?
Elvis Parsley.
Abcjojo

Why was the skeleton scared to go on the roller coaster?
Because he didn't have the guts!
Happyplum55

What do you call a fairy that doesn't take baths?
Stinkerbell!
091098a

What do you call a vampire that lives in the kitchen?
Spatula!
Aedaniswicked

What's pink?
A colour!
Gabe-o

What do cannibals do at weddings?
Toast the bride and groom.
Emmorock

What do you get if you cross a vampire and a snowman?
Frostbite!
Haggisface2000

49

More Knock, Knocks

Knock, knock.
Who's there?
Madame.
Madame who?
Madame monster fingers are stuck in the keyhole!

Yoyomaisie123

Knock, knock.
Who's there?
Katsuma.
Katsuma who?
Knock, knock.
Who's there?
Katsuma.
Katsuma who?
Knock, knock.
Who's there?
Furi.
Furi who?
I'll bet your Furi glad I didn't say Katsuma!

Vasa12345

Knock, knock.
Who's there?
Roary Scrawl.
Roary Scrawl who?
Roary's crawling on the floor trying to find his eyeballs!
Lila123123

Knock, knock.
Who's there?
I'm going to eat.
I'm going to eat who?
I'm going to eat you!
Bobbieheather

Knock, knock.
Who's there?
Knock, knock?
Who's there?
Knock, knock.
Who's there?
A Moshling who can't reach the doorbell!
Fishy09

What is brown and hairy and wears sunglasses?
Furi on holiday!
Taylortwilight030900

What did one Furi say to the other Furi?
I've no idea, I don't speak Furi!
Meerkatad123

What time is it when Furi sits on your fence?
Time to get a new fence!
Hanbear4

Where do you find Furi snails?
At the end of Furi's fingers!
Womble27

Moshling Guffaws

What does Purdy eat for breakfast?
Mice krispies!
Shadow8668

Why did Burnie walk across the road?
Because his wings were tired.
Tanon

What's Kissy's favourite play?
Romeo and Ghouliet!
Creamraspberrys

What did Cleo say when she woke up?
I want my mummy!
ILS23

How can you tell if Fifi has been in your fridge?
She leaves footprints in the butter!
Littleprincess000

What did Scamp say when he sat on the sandpaper?

Grrr, rough, rough, rough!

Puffy-choochoo

What is Lady Meowford's favourite colour?

Purrr-ple.

Paigy16

How do you stop Big Bad Bill from charging?

Take away his credit card!

meekestar

Why did Prof. Purplex cross the road?

To invent the other side!

Babybella9124

Monster Cracks

What's a monster's favourite bit of *The Daily Growl* newspaper?
The horror-scopes!
Kwitina

What do you get if you put a Moshi Monster in a blender?
A mushy monster!
Redgreen12345678910

What do you call a monster with eight eyes, four mouths and seven ears?
Ugly!
Purple101722

Where do you find a one-legged monster?
Wherever you left it!
Taylorblue308

If my monster Ron had twenty apples in his right hand and thirty apples in his left hand, what would he have?

Very big hands!

Spike9302

What do you get if you cross monsters with dogs?

A neighbourhood without any cats!

Violetcrumble101

What do you call a smart, cool, good-looking, friendly monster?

A rumour!

Peachyshrooms

Why did the monster take a pencil to bed?

So he could draw the curtains!

Dazliquid

Zommer Side-Splitters

What does it say on Zommer's tombstone?
Rest in Pieces!
Mad_donkey

What is Zommer's favourite tree?
A cemetery!
Rosiechap

Do Zommers have trouble getting dates?
No, they usually manage to dig someone up!
Trixxirox

What does Zommer like to eat?
Ghoulash!
Oupp

Why did Zommer spit out the clown?
Because he tasted funny!
Puffy-choochoo

Why are Zommers such good fun?
Because they have you in stitches!
Lolliepopsie

How did the eldery Zommer cross the road?
He used a Zommerframe!
Championswimmer

Why won't Zommer ask Poppet to dance?
He doesn't have the guts!
Sheri

Moshling Mockery

How does Ecto start a race?
Ready, steady, glow!
Sunsetsmilles

Why was Cali embarrassed?
Because she saw the boat's bottom!
Squishy7000

Can Mr Snoodle jump higher than a two-storey house?
Of course, houses can't jump!
Raja26

Why does Stanley the Songful Seahorse live in salt water?
Because pepper makes him sneeze!
Babybz

How does Prof. Purplex get out of his nest?
He uses the eggs-it!
Hettyfeather3490

How does Peppy the Stunt Penguin fix his house?
Igloos it together!
Coolala8890

What happened to White Fang when he ate Mini Ben?
He got ticks!
Wazupbro

What does ShiShi pack for her holidays?
Just the bear necessities!
Princessmeg1999

Why is Kissy bad at telling lies?
Because you can see right through her!
Partybettyboo

Final Furi Funnies

What's Furi's favourite vegetable?
Sa-SQUASH!
Dootus

Why do Furi's have fur coats?
Because they'd look silly wearing rain macs!
Suzzane00800

What do you call Furi in a phone box?
Stuck!
Selgomez2010

What is furry, grumpy and rolling?
A Furi falling down the stairs!

What's furry, grumpy and laughing?
The Furi that pushed it!
Sweetsugar67

Doctor, doctor, my hair keeps falling out. Can you give me anything to keep it in?

Doctor: Yes, here's a paper bag!
Bluedawg

What would you get if you crossed a Furi with a kangeroo?
A fur coat with big pockets!
Coco2000419

What do the monsters sing on Furi's birthday?
Fur he's a jolly good fellow!
April4kate9

LAST MINUTE LAUGHS

What's Roary Scrawl's favourite food?
Eye pie!
Redracheld

Why did Banana Montana go to the doctor's?
Because she wasn't peeling well!
Glaceon57

Why don't monsters eat penguins?
Because they can't get the wrappers off!
Magnet

What do monsters like with their fish and chips?
Moshi peas!
Beehag